LAUGH OUT LOUD!

THE MONSTER FUN JOKE BOOK

Sean Connolly and Kay Barnham

WINDMILL
BOOKS

New York

Published in 2012 by Windmill Books, LLC
303 Park Avenue South, Suite # 1280, New York, NY 10010-3657

First Edition

Editor: Joe Harris
Illustrations: Adam Clay and Dynamo Design
Layout Design: Notion Design

Library of Congress Cataloging-in-Publication Data

Connolly, Sean, 1956–
  The monster fun joke book / by Sean Connolly and Kay Barnham. — 1st ed.
      p. cm. — (Laugh out loud!)
  Includes index.
  ISBN 978-1-61533-360-8 (library binding) — ISBN 978-1-61533-398-1 (pbk.) — ISBN 978-1-61533-462-9
(6-pack)
  1. Monsters—Juvenile humor. I. Barnham, Kay. II. Title.
  PN6231.M665C66 2012
  808.8'037—dc22
                                        2010052139
Printed in China

For more great fiction and nonfiction, go to www.windmillbooks.com

CPSIA Compliance Information: Batch #AS2011WM: For Further Information contact Windmill Books, New York, New York at 1-866-478-0556
SL001831US

CONTENTS

MONSTER FUN

Where do ghosts swim?
In the Dead Sea.

What did the vampire doctor say?
Necks please!

Did you hear about the banshee who wanted to be an actress?
She did a scream test.

What does a dragon call knights in armor?
Canned food!

What do you get if you cross a vampire and a circus entertainer ?
Someone who goes straight for the juggler!

What do you get if you cross a vampire with a mummy?
Something you wouldn't want to unwrap!

What do ghosts eat for dinner?
Goulash!

How do ghosts begin business letters?
"Tomb it may concern..."

Why didn't the skeleton fight the monster?
He didn't have the guts!

What has a pointy hat, a broomstick and a blue face?
A witch holding her breath.

MONSTER FUN

How can you tell when there's a giant monster under your bed?
When your nose touches the ceiling.

What happened to the vampire with bad breath?
His dentist told him to gargoyle twice a day!

What do vampires do at eleven o'clock every night?
They have a coffin break.

What was written on the robot's tombstone?
Rust in pieces!

How does Frankenstein's monster sit in a chair?
Bolt upright!

MONSTER FUN

How do you know that smoking is harmful to your health?
Well, look what happened to all the dragons!

Should monsters eat people on an empty stomach?
No, they should eat them on a plate!

What is monsters' favorite party game?
Swallow the leader!

Why don't skeletons sing church music?
They have no organs.

What goes "WOO-HA-HA" THUMP?
Frankenstein's monster laughing his head off.

MONSTER FUN

What job does Dracula have with the Transylvanian baseball team?
He looks after the bats!

Why do ghosts never feel guilty?
They have a clear conscience!

First friend: Did you know that you can get fur from a vampire?
Second friend: Really? What kind of fur?
First friend: As fur away as possible!

Why do vampires dislike computers?
They hate anything new-fang-led!

Why did the car stop when it saw the monster truck?
It had a nervous breakdown.

Why was young Dr. Frankenstein so popular?
Because he was great at making new friends!

How did you know I was a ghost?
Oh, I can see right through you!

How did the ghostly teacher make sure his pupils had learned what he had written on the board?
He went through it again!

Why did the monster buy an ax?
Because he wanted to get a-head in life!

How do vampires get clean?
In a blood bath!

What do trainee witches do at school?
Spelling tests.

What is the name for a group of vampires?
A fang club!

Why are vampires good at treating people with coughs?
Because they can clear your throat in seconds!

How do big, hairy monsters eat their dinner?
They wolf it down!

Why did the two vampire bats get married?
Because they were heels over heads in love!

MONSTER FUN

Why do ghosts go back to the same place every year for their vacation?
They like their old haunts best!

Did you hear about the hip-hop mummy?
He was a wrap artist!

What do the police call it when they watch a vampire's house?
A stake out!

Where did Dracula open his bank account?
At a blood bank!

What will a vampire never order in a restaurant?
Steak.

MONSTER FUN

Why wasn't the werewolf astronaut allowed to land his spaceship?
Because the moon was full!

Who do vampires invite to their birthday parties?
Anybody they can dig up!

Why did Dracula advertise for a housekeeper?
He wanted some new blood in the house!

Who is the world's scariest superhero?
Vampire bat-man!

What sort of telescope lets you see ghosts?
A horrorscope!

What do you call a lazy skeleton?
Bone idle!

What did Frankenstein do when the monster's head kept falling off?
He made a bolt for it!

Why do monsters like to stand in a ring?
They love being part of a vicious circle!

Where do werewolves live?
In warehouses.

Why doesn't Dracula have any friends?
Because he's a pain in the neck!

What does Dracula drink?
"De-coffin-ated" coffee!

"Hurry up," said the father skeleton to his son, "or you'll be late for the skull bus!"

What do you call a kind, helpful monster who likes flowers and butterflies?
A failure!

What did the old vampire say when he broke his teeth?
Fangs for the memory...

What does it say on the mummy's garage entrance?
Toot, and come in!

MONSTER FUN

Who was the winner of the headless horse race?
No one. They all finished neck and neck!

Why are you throwing garlic out of the window?
To keep vampires away.
But there aren't any vampires here.
See—it works!

Why did the giant robot feel sick after eating a train?
He caught a commuter virus!

If having hairy palms is the first sign of turning into a monster, what is the second?
Looking for them!

Why did Godzilla stop eating buildings?
He got atomic ache!

MONSTER FUN

What do ghosts do if they are afraid?
Hide under a sheet!

Why did the monster have twins in his lunchbox?
In case he felt like seconds!

Why didn't the vampire laugh at the joke about the wooden stake?
He didn't get the point!

Why did the werewolf swallow a bag full of pennies?
Because he thought the change would do him good!

Why do zombies always look so tired?
They are dead on their feet!

What is the first thing a monster eats when he goes to a restaurant?
The waiter!

What do monsters call a crowded swimming pool?
Soup!

Why did the robot need a manicure?
He had rusty nails!

Why didn't the phantom win the lottery?
He didn't have a ghost of a chance!

Why do football teams have to practice so much when they play against zombies?
Because they face stiff competition!

What did the young ghost call his mom and dad?
His trans-parents!

Why do little monsters not mind being eaten by ghosts?
Because they know they will always be in good spirits!

Why are there more ghost cats than ghost dogs?
Because every cat has nine lives!

Why do monster parents tell their children to eat cabbage?
Because they want them to have a healthy green complexion!

MONSTER FUN

Which monster is the most untidy?
The Loch Mess Monster!

Why did the cyclops school close down?
Because they only had one pupil!

Why are vampires stupid?
Because blood is thicker than water!

Why do other monsters find mummies vain?
They're so wrapped up in themselves.

Why do vampires never invite trolls to their dinner parties?
They can't stand all that goblin!

MONSTER FUN

What do you call a ghostly chicken?
A poultry-geist.

Why did the zombie go to the pharmacy?
He wanted something to help stop his coffin.

What do you call a kid vampire?
A pain in the knee!

Who do vampires invite to their weddings?
All their blood relatives!

How does a skeleton know when it's going to rain?
He just gets a feeling in his bones!

Why don't ghosts do aerobics?
Because they don't want to be exorcised!

Why are owls so brave at night?
Because they don't give a hoot for ghosts, monsters, or vampires!

How do vampires show affection for each other?
They bat their eyelids!

What is the first thing you should put into a haunted house?
Someone else!

Why did Goldilocks go to Egypt?
She wanted to see the mummy bear!

What did the werewolf say to the skeleton?
It's been so nice getting to gnaw you!

Why did the ghost go to the bicycle shop?
He needed some new spooks for his front wheel!

What do you get if you cross the Abominable Snowman and Count Dracula?
Severe frostbite!

What did the witch call her baby daughter?
Wanda!

What do you need to pick up a giant's silverware?
A forklift.

MONSTER FUN

What do you call a male vampire in women's clothing?
Drag-cula!

How do you make a skeleton laugh?
Just tickle his funny bone.

Knock knock!
Who's there?
Russia!
Russia who?
Russia way—a monster's coming!

Why was the genie in the lamp angry?
Someone rubbed him up the wrong way!

MONSTER FUN

What do you get if you cross a warlock and a laptop?
A computer wizard!

What do skeletons say before eating?
Bone appetite!

What do you call the jewels that ghosts wear?
Tombstones!

What do dinosaurs rest their teacups on?
Tyrannosaucers.

MONSTER FUN

How do you help Frankenstein's monster?
Give him a hand when he needs it!

How do witch children listen to stories?
Spellbound!

How can you tell
when a robot
is angry?
It flips its lid!

What flavor drink do
monsters slurp?
Lemon and slime.

Book spotted at the
school library:
"The Haunted House," by Hugo First.

What do you call a hairy monster that's lost
its way home?
A where-am-I wolf.

What happens when a witch catches the flu?
Everyone gets a cold spell!

Why do vampires have a steady nerve?
They are as ghoul as cucumbers!

Why don't vampires write their own books?
They prefer to use ghost writers!

Where do monsters like to go on vacation?
Death Valley!

MONSTER FUN

Why do sea monsters go to so many parties?
Because they always have a whale of a time!

What do you call monster children?
Ghouls and boils.

How did the mother monster stop her son from biting his nails?
She cut his fingers off.

Mommy, mommy, what is a werewolf?
Be quiet and comb your face!

What do abominable snowmen sing at parties?
"Freeze a jolly good fellow..."

MONSTER FUN

Why are monsters forgetful?
Because everything goes in one ear and out the others.

What do baby sea monsters play with?
Doll-fins!

What happened when the Abominable Snowman ate chili con carne?
He blew his cool.

What is a vampire's favorite animal?
A giraffe.

What do mummies do to relax?
They just unwind a little!

Why can you never get through to a vampire bat on the telephone?
Because they always hang up!

Why did King Kong climb the Empire State Building in New York City?
He wanted to catch a plane.

What kind of mistakes do young ghosts make at school?
Boo-boos.

What was the name of the ghost who ate too much porridge?
Ghoul-dilocks.

Why are so few ghosts ever arrested?
Because it's so hard to pin anything on them.

MONSTER FUN

What do you call a
little monster with a
wooden leg?
A hoblin-goblin.

Why are vampires
such good
comedians?
Because of their
biting wit.

What happened to
the naughtiest witch
in the class?
She was ex-spelled!

Which monster has the best hearing?
That depends on which one is the eeriest.

Why don't witches wear sombreros?
Because there's no point.

MONSTER FUN

What pets does Dracula own?
A bloodhound and a ghoul-fish!

What happened to the ghostly comedian?
He was booed off the stage.

What happened to the ghost who got lost in the fog?
He is now sadly mist.

Why do skeletons hate winter?
Because the cold goes right through them!

Why did King Kong join the army?
To learn about gorilla warfare.

Glossary

aerobics (uh-ROH-biks) exercises that keep your body in shape

atomic (ah-TOM-ik) to do with atoms, the basic unit that everything is made from – or the energy that comes from atoms

banshee (BAN-shee) a wailing spirit from Irish folk tales

complexion (kom-PLEK-shun) the way the skin of your face looks

exorcise (EX-or-size) to drive a ghost or spirit away from a place

goulash (GOO-lahsh) a meat and vegetable soup from Hungary

Further Reading

Dahl, Michael. *Screaming with Laughter*. Mankato, MN: Picture Window Books, 2010.

Horsfall, Jacqueline. *Giggle Fit: Dinosaur Jokes*. New York: Sterling Publishing, 2004.

Winter, Judy A. *Jokes About Monsters*. Mankato, MN: Capstone Press, 2010.

Index

Web Sites

For Web resources related to the subject of this book, go to: www.windmillbooks.com/weblinks and select this book's title.